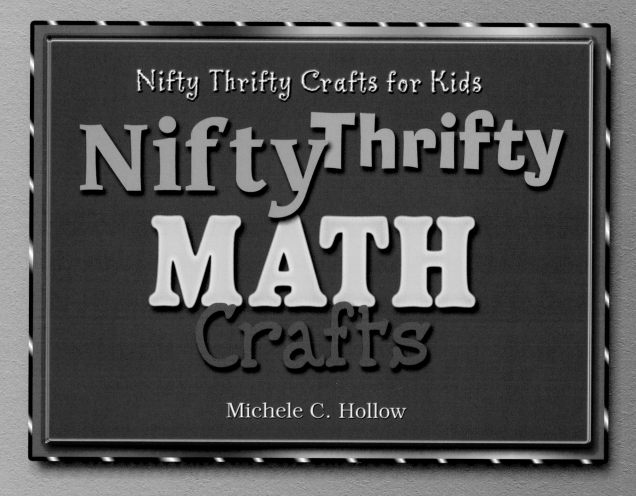

Nifty Thrifty Crafts for Kids

Nifty Thrifty

MATH

Crafts

Michele C. Hollow

Enslow Elementary

an imprint of

Enslow Publishers, Inc.

40 Industrial Road
Box 398
Berkeley Heights, NJ 07922
USA

http://www.enslow.com

Enslow Elementary, an imprint of Enslow Publishers, Inc.

Enslow Elementary® is a registered trademark of Enslow Publishers, Inc.

Library of Congress Cataloging-in-Publication Data

Hollow, Michele C.

   Nifty thrifty crafts for kids. Nifty thrifty math crafts / Michele C. Hollow.—1st ed.
     p. cm.
   Includes bibliographical references and index.
   ISBN-13: 978-0-7660-2781-7
   ISBN-10: 0-7660-2781-3
    1. Handicraft—Juvenile literature. 2. Mathematics in art—Juvenile literature. I. Title. II. Title: Nifty thrifty
math crafts.
   TT160.H523 2007
   745.5—dc22   2006018294

Printed in the United States of America

10 9 8 7 6 5 4 3 2 1

To Our Readers: We have done our best to make sure all Internet Addresses in this book were active and appropriate when we went to press. However, the author and the publisher have no control over and assume no liability for the material available on those Internet sites or on other Web sites they may link to. Any comments or suggestions can be sent by e-mail to comments@enslow.com or to the address on the back cover.

Every effort has been made to locate all copyright holders of material used in this book. If any errors or omissions have occurred, corrections will be made in future editions of this book.

Illustration Credits: Crafts prepared by June Ponte; photography by Nicole diMella/Enslow Publishers, Inc.; Shutterstock, pp. 4, 5.

Cover Credits: Photography by Nicole diMella/Enslow Publishers, Inc.

Safety Note: Be sure to ask for help from an adult, if needed, to complete these crafts!

Contents

Math!

Knowing how to use a ruler and subtract a few inches from a rectangle to make it a square comes in handy when you decorate your room. Division is important, especially when you are dividing slices of pie or sharing a box of cookies. Math is a skill we use each and every day.

Did you know that math is the only language shared by all human beings? It does not matter if you are in the United States or living in Europe, China, or Africa. Even though we use different forms of money, addition skills are the same throughout the world.

Mathematics is a universal language. It is not a language like English, Spanish, or French. It is a system of numbers that people from all over the globe can understand. The language

4

of mathematics is called numeracy. This universal language helps scientists develop new formulas to fight disease. Bakers use math to create delicious cakes and cookies. They need to know just the right amounts of flour, eggs, and sugar to make a tasty  dessert. Interior designers need to know how many rolls of wallpaper or how many quarts of paint to buy when decorating a room. Athletes use math to calculate distances. Artists also use math when creating sculptures or paintings.

All of the projects in this book combine math with art. You can do many of these activities by yourself or you can ask an adult for help. You and your friends can work on a few of these projects together.

Have fun while you are busy dividing, subtracting, multiplying, and adding supplies for each project.

Count On It Piggy Bank

A personal piggy bank is a great way to learn about numbers. You can put a percentage of your allowance into your bank. Your goal may be to buy a video game or book. Or see how much money you can save in a year. You can practice adding and subtracting sums as you save and withdraw money from your bank.

- ✔ **empty coffee can or other container with a plastic lid**
- ✔ **tissue paper in various colors**
- ✔ **water**
- ✔ **white glue**
- ✔ **paper bowl**
- ✔ **small paintbrush**
- ✔ **stickers (optional)**
- ✔ **glitter (optional)**
- ✔ **fabric scrap**
- ✔ **pencil**
- ✔ **scissors**
- ✔ **notebook**

1. Remove the label from a coffee can. Wash and dry the can.

2. Tear pieces of tissue paper into 2-inch, 3-inch, and 4-inch pieces. Edges can be rough.

3. Pour 1/8 cup of water into a paper bowl and add 1/2 cup of glue to make a glue wash. Stir.

4. Brush a small amount of the glue wash onto the tissue paper pieces and place onto the can. Overlap the pieces. Let dry. If you wish, glue glitter or place stickers on top of the tissue paper.

5. Place the lid on a scrap of fabric and trace around it with a pencil. Cut out the circle shape. Glue the fabric to the top of the lid. Let dry.

6. Open the lid each time you want to deposit or withdraw money from your bank. Use a notebook to keep track of your money. Write down the total you first put into the bank. Add or subtract the amounts as you put money in or take money out.

My Age Kite

Are You Ready?

How old are you? How about making a kite using your age? This craft will be shown as if you are nine years old. It can be made using any number—whether you are eight, nine, or even thirteen years old.

Wait for a windy day to take your kite outside to fly it. Hold the yarn in your hand and run while gently tossing the kite up into the air. If the wind is just right, it will stay up.

Get Set

- ✔ **markers**
- ✔ **brown paper bag (lunch size)**
- ✔ **ruler**
- ✔ **ribbons of different colors**
- ✔ **white glue**
- ✔ **yarn**
- ✔ **masking tape**

Let's Go!

1. Use markers to write your age that many times on a clean brown paper lunch bag (see A). If you are nine years old, write the number nine, nine times (see B).

2. Use a ruler to measure and cut four 9-inch pieces of ribbon. If you are eight years old, measure and cut four 8-inch pieces of ribbon; if you are 10 years old, four 10-inch pieces; and so forth.

3. Glue the ribbons to the four open corners of the bag. Let dry.

4. Make a handle for the kite. Add your age to itself. For example, $9 + 9 = 18$. Measure and cut an 18-inch piece of yarn.

5. Place one end of the yarn inside the bag, on the side, about 1 inch from the edge. Attach with masking tape. Do the same with the other end of the yarn, on the other side (see C).

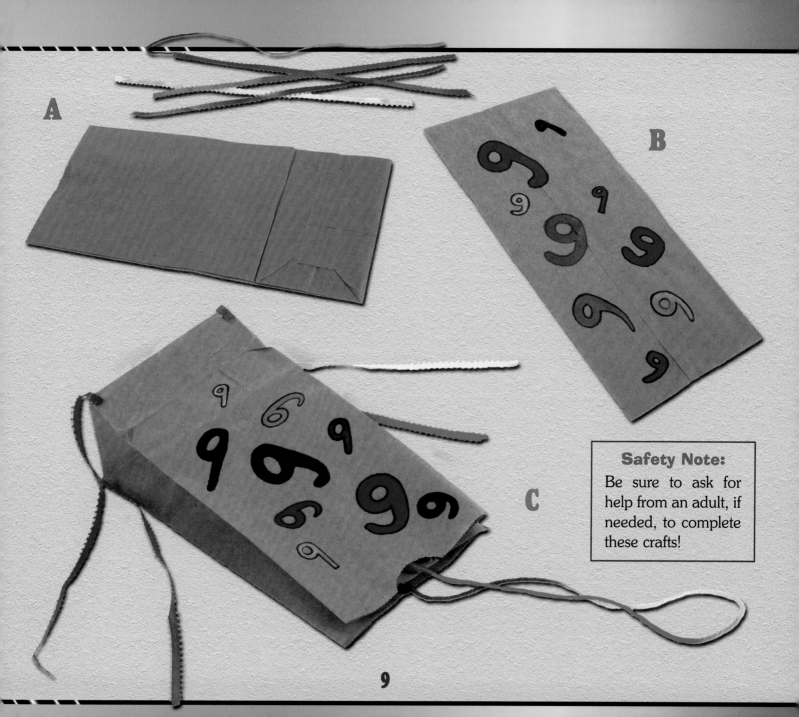

A

B

C

Origami Hat

Origami is the ancient art of paper folding. It originated in Japan thousands of years ago. It is still widely practiced throughout Asia and in the United States—as well as in other parts of the world. This is a basic pattern that can be decorated to your liking.

Get Set

✔ **newspaper page**

✔ **markers (optional)**

✔ **glitter glue (optional)**

Let's Go!

1. Tear out one page from a newspaper. It must be a rectangle (see A).

2. Fold the top edge down to meet the bottom edge. Fold the rectangle in half so it looks like a book. Unfold back to a rectangle. You should have a crease in the center of the rectangle.

3. Fold two triangles by bringing the top corners together in the middle to meet (see B). Notice the shapes of these two right angle triangles.

4. Fold the two overlapping strips on the bottom up—one on one side and one on the other. They will look like long rectangles. If you wish, decorate the origami hat with markers and glitter glue (see C). Open at the bottom and place on your head.

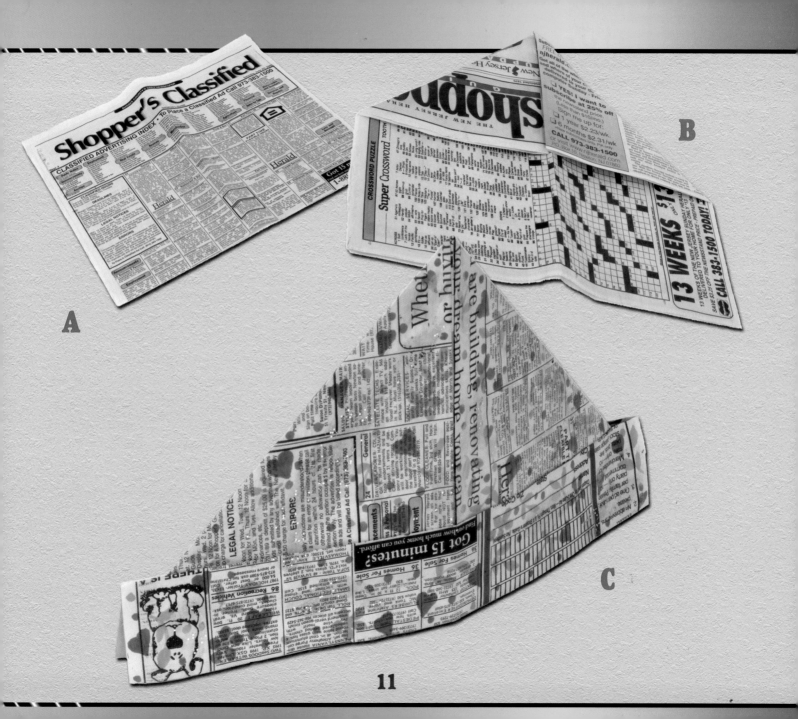

Dream Catcher Clock

Are You Ready?

Hundreds of years ago, some American Indians hung dream catchers over the cradles of their children. They believed the dream catcher would catch the bad dreams and let the good ones pass through. Today, they are still created for this purpose and as works of art too.

Get Set

- ✔ **9-inch paper plate**
- ✔ **scissors**
- ✔ **pencil**
- ✔ **12 brass fasteners**
- ✔ **marker**
- ✔ **ball of yarn**
- ✔ **ruler**

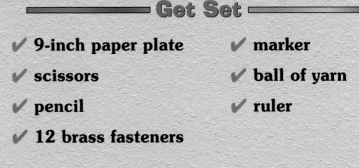

Let's Go!

1. Use scissors to carefully poke a hole in the middle of the paper plate and cut out the entire center, leaving a 1-1/2 inch rim (see A).

2. With a pencil, lightly make evenly spaced dots around the rim like a clock.

3. Make a hole with the brass fasteners by carefully pushing them through each of the dots. Separate the tabs of the brass fasteners under the paper plate rim. Use a marker to write the clock numbers around the rim (see B).

4. Measure and cut six 9-inch pieces of yarn. Tie the end of one piece of yarn around the brass fastener at 12. Tie the other end around the brass fastener at 6 (see C). Tie another piece of yarn at 1, and tie the other end at 7. Continue in this pattern until all pieces of yarn have been used.

5. Cut a 6-inch piece of yarn. Tie both ends together around the back of the top brass fastener. Your dream catcher clock is ready to hang (see D).

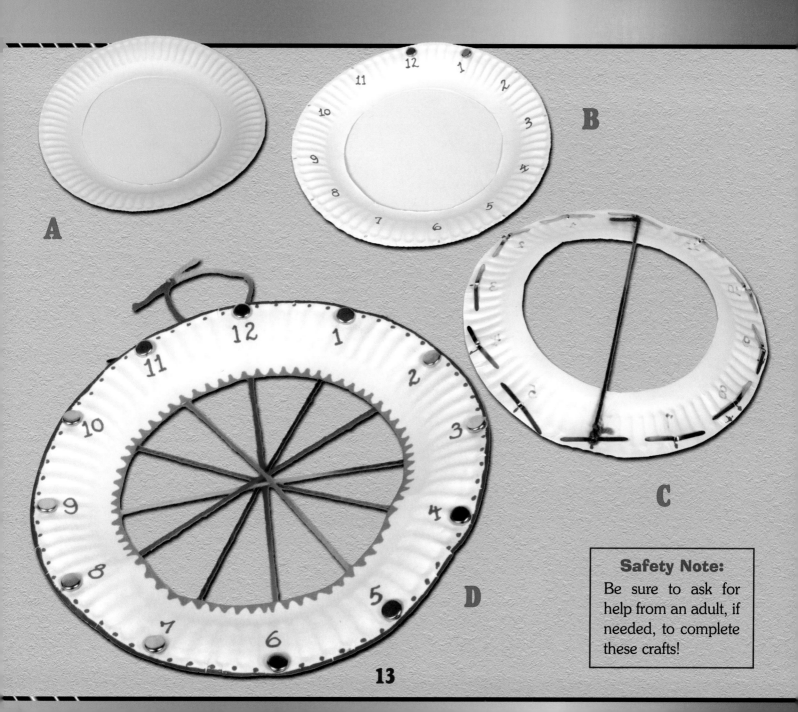

A

B

C

D

Safety Note:
Be sure to ask for help from an adult, if needed, to complete these crafts!

13

Equilateral Triangle Picture Frame

Are You Ready?

All of the sides of an equilateral triangle are the same length. You can take a ruler to measure each side. How about making a square inside a triangle?

Let's Go!

1. Cut two equilateral triangles, with all three sides measuring 6 inches, out of construction paper, felt, or craft foam. (See page 26 for the pattern.)

Get Set

- ✔ **construction paper, felt, or craft foam**
- ✔ **pencil**
- ✔ **ruler**
- ✔ **scissors**
- ✔ **photograph (Ask permission first!)**
- ✔ **white glue**
- ✔ **small piece of yarn**

2. Take one triangle and measure a 2-inch square (all four sides should measure 2 inches) in the center. Carefully cut out the square.

3. Place the triangle with the cutout on top of the other, and slide your photo in between.

4. Remove the top triangle. Glue your photo to the solid triangle. Let dry. Glue the top triangle over the photo. Let dry.

5. Make a loop out of a short piece of yarn. Glue both ends on the back of the triangle at the top. Let dry.

Stegosaurus-Shape Shadow Puppet

Did you know that stegosaurus means plated reptile? The mighty stegosaurus was a giant plant eater the size of an army tank. To cast a giant stegosaurus shadow on a wall, hold the puppet's stick in one hand and shine a flashlight facing the puppet.

Get Set

✔ **2 9-inch paper plates**

✔ **scissors**

✔ **ruler**

✔ **marker**

✔ **white glue**

✔ **clear tape**

✔ **unsharpened pencil**

Let's Go!

1. Cut a paper plate in half. One half is the stegosaurus body.

2. On the other half of the paper plate and on the second paper plate, measure and cut three 2-inch diamonds, two 1-1/2 inch equilateral triangles, two 2-inch rectangular boot shapes for the feet, and one 2-1/2 inch narrow strip for the tail. For the head, cut out a 3-inch rectangle from the second plate (see A). (See page 26 for the pattern.)

3. Glue one diamond to the center of the rim of the paper plate half. Measure 3 inches to the left of the center diamond. Glue on one diamond. Measure 3 inches to the right of the center diamond and glue on another diamond. Let dry.

4. Glue one triangle between the first two diamonds on the rim. Glue the other triangle in between the last two diamonds (see B). Glue the feet at the bottom and the tail at one end. Let dry.

5. At the opposite end of the tail, glue the head to the body. Let dry.

6. If you wish, decorate the dinosaur. Tape an unsharpened pencil to the bottom center on the back of the dinosaur (see C).

A

B

C

Roman Numeral Secret Message

Are You Ready?

Roman numerals are expressed by letters of the alphabet. You can use Roman numerals to write a secret note and send to a friend. When you add Roman numerals, think in terms of everyday numbers. Since you know that V equals 5 and X equals 10, just add 5 and 10 to get 15, which is XV in Roman numerals.

I = 1	C = 100
V = 5	D = 500
X = 10	M = 1,000
L = 50	

Get Set

- ✔ **brown paper bag**
- ✔ **scissors (optional)**
- ✔ **pencil**
- ✔ **ruler**
- ✔ **marker (optional)**
- ✔ **scrap paper**
- ✔ **yarn**

Let's Go!

1. Tear or cut a brown paper bag into an 8-inch × 12-inch piece (see A).

2. With a pencil and ruler draw a 7-inch × 7-inch square on the top 3/4 of the brown paper. Make a grid inside the square with ten squares going up and ten squares going across. (See page 27 for the pattern.)

3. Use Roman numerals to number the squares on the left side, on the outside of the squares. Start with I at the bottom and end with X at the top. Use Roman numerals to number the squares on the bottom, on the outside of the squares. Start with I on the left and end with X.

4. In the squares of the grid, write the alphabet. Put one letter in a square. Make sure to jumble the letters up and use a letter only once (see B). If you wish, go over all the pencil lines with a marker.

5. Now to make a secret message! What would you like to tell your friend? Write your message on a piece of scrap paper. Use the grid to make your coded message. Find the first letter of your message. What row (across) is it in? Use the Roman numerals on the bottom for the first part of your set. What column (up) is the letter in? Use the Roman numerals on the left for the second part of your set. Write the set in parentheses on the bottom of the brown paper. What is the second letter of your message? Use the same "across and up" method for each letter of your message (see C).

6. When you are done with your message, carefully roll up the brown paper and tie a piece of yarn around it (see D). Give it to your friend. Give him or her a hint and say, "Across and up." Let your friend decode!

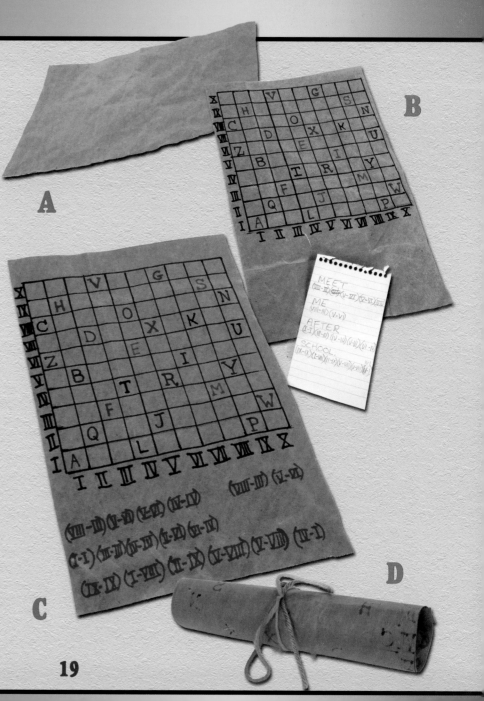

19

Coin Pouch

Are You Ready?

Here is a neat pouch where you can keep your change. Made out of a juice pouch, it holds your coins so you always know where they are. You will need math to measure how much cord to use and for cutting.

Get Set

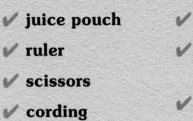

- ✔ juice pouch
- ✔ ruler
- ✔ scissors
- ✔ cording
- ✔ hole punch
- ✔ hook-and-loop fabr fasteners
- ✔ white glue

Let's Go!

1. Make sure a juice pouch is empty (see A). Measure and cut across 1/2 inch from the top of the juice pouch.

2. Clean and dry the juice pouch.

3. Cut a 28-inch length of cord. Use a hole punch to punch out two holes, one on each corner of the juice pouch near the top. Slide the cord through the holes and knot in place (see B).

4. Cut two pieces of hook and loop fabric fasteners—about 3 inches each.

5. Open the pouch and glue the two pieces of hook-and-loop fabric fasteners across from each other near the inside top of the opening. Let dry (see C).

6. You are ready to fill your pouch with coins. How many coins do you have? What are they worth? You can add and subtract coins from the total.

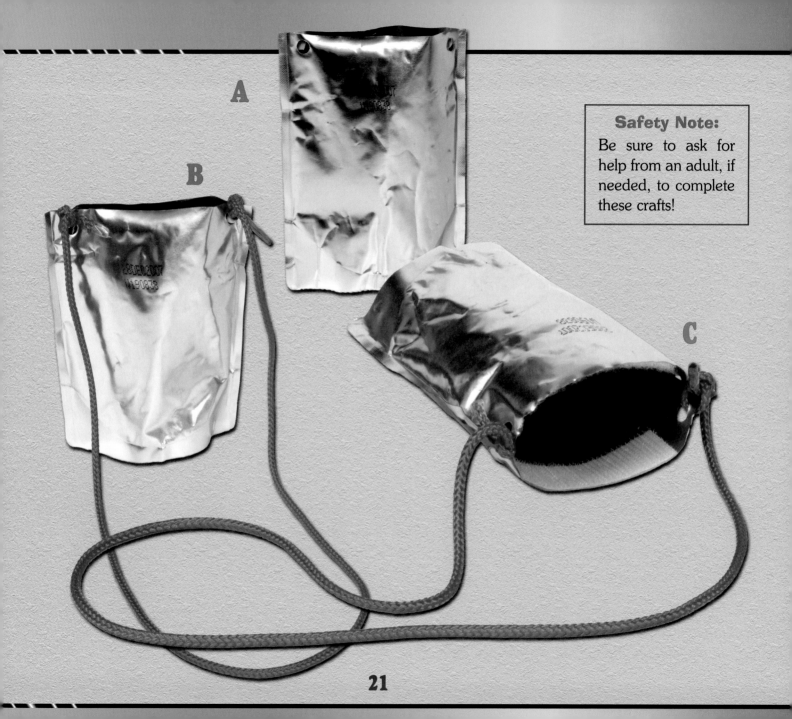

A

B

C

Tessellation Cube Weight

A tessellation is a repeating pattern of shapes that fit together. A mosaic tile pattern, like one you might find on a floor, is a tessellation. Make this cube paperweight that is covered in different tessellations.

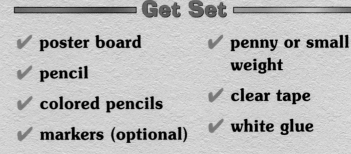

✔ **poster board**

✔ **pencil**

✔ **colored pencils**

✔ **markers (optional)**

✔ **penny or small weight**

✔ **clear tape**

✔ **white glue**

Let's Go!

1. On a piece of poster board, use a pencil to make a cube pattern (see A). (See page 29 for the pattern.)

2. With a pencil, make a dot grid on each of the outer sides of the cube. Each square side should have a grid. Each grid should have the same number of dots going across and up.

3. Connect the dots. (See page 29 for the pattern.) What kind of tessellations, or repeating patterns, can you make? Try a different pattern on each side of the cube (see B). Use colored pencils or markers to fill in the patterns.

4. Cut out the cube pattern (see C). Fold the sides to form the cube. Place a small amount of white glue on the tabs. Close the cube. If you wish, use clear tape instead of glue to close the cube.

5. Turn the cube over. Tape a penny or small weight to the bottom of the cube (see D).

6. Your tessellation cube weight is ready to hold down a stack of papers. What other tessellations can you come up with?

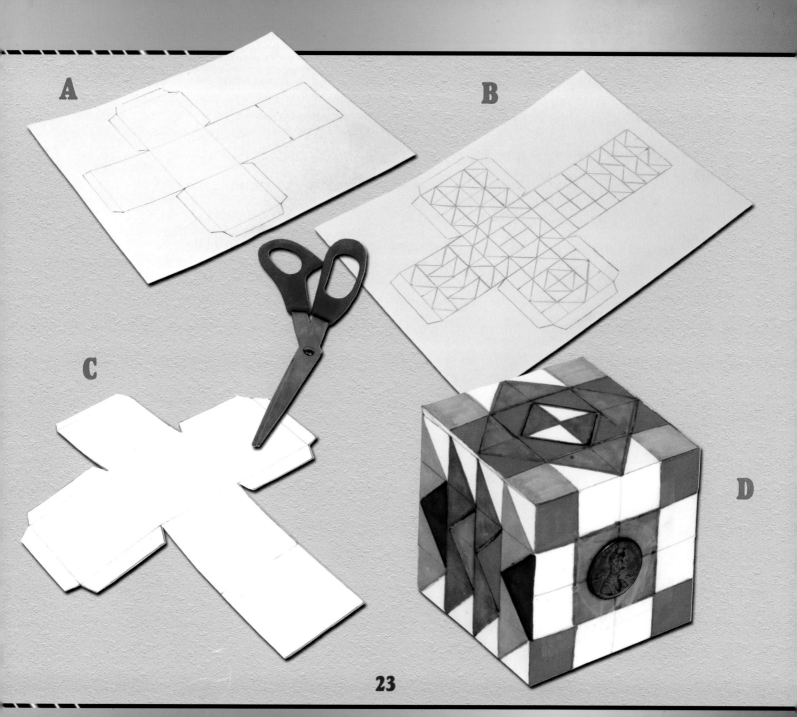

A

B

C

D

Symmetrical Butterfly

Are You Ready?

Two halves are symmetrical if they mirror each other exactly. If they do not, they are asymmetrical. In this craft, the two wings on the butterfly are mirror images of each other.

Get Set

✔ **construction paper**

✔ **pencil or marker**

✔ **scissors**

✔ **white glue**

✔ **glitter (optional)**

Let's Go!

1. Fold one piece of construction paper in half. Starting at the top of the fold, draw a wiggly butterfly-wing shape. (See page 28 for the pattern.)

2. Cut along the wiggle line and open the paper. There are two exact halves (see A).

3. Take another sheet of construction paper and fold it in half. Draw one small circle, one small diamond, and one small square. Cut out the shapes. You will have two of each (see B).

4. Glue one set of shapes on one side of the butterfly. Glue the second set of shapes exactly opposite the first set, on the other side of the butterfly (see C). Let dry. If you wish, add glitter. Let dry.

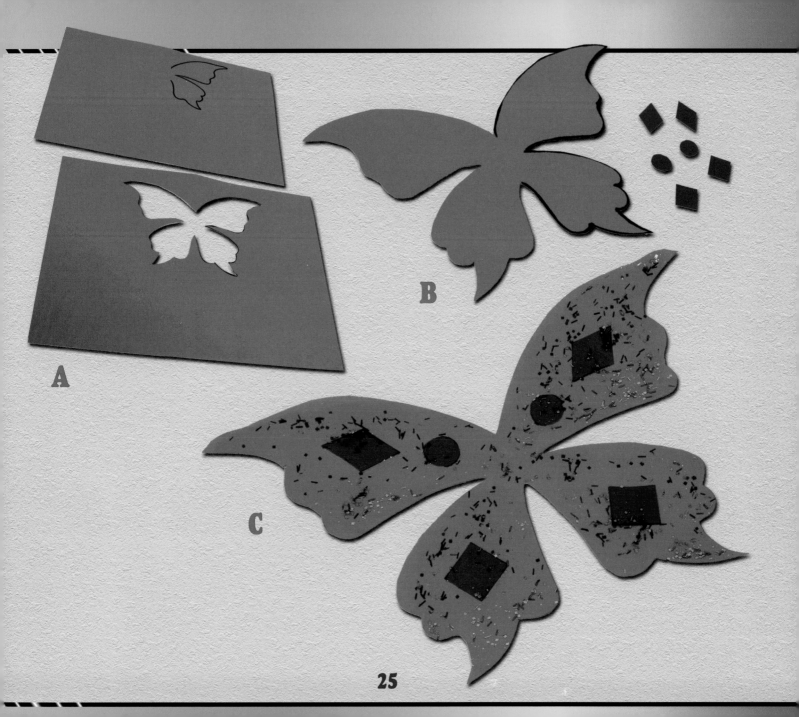

A

B

C

Patterns

Use tracing paper to copy the patterns on these pages. Ask an adult to help you cut and trace the shapes onto construction paper.

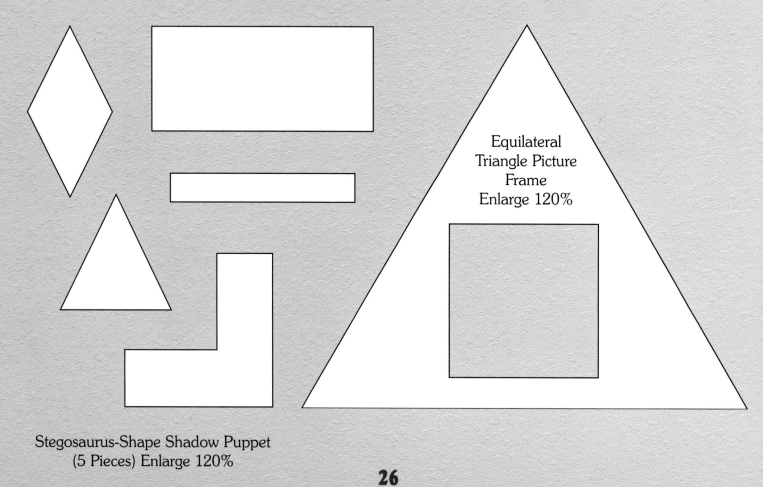

Equilateral
Triangle Picture
Frame
Enlarge 120%

Stegosaurus-Shape Shadow Puppet
(5 Pieces) Enlarge 120%

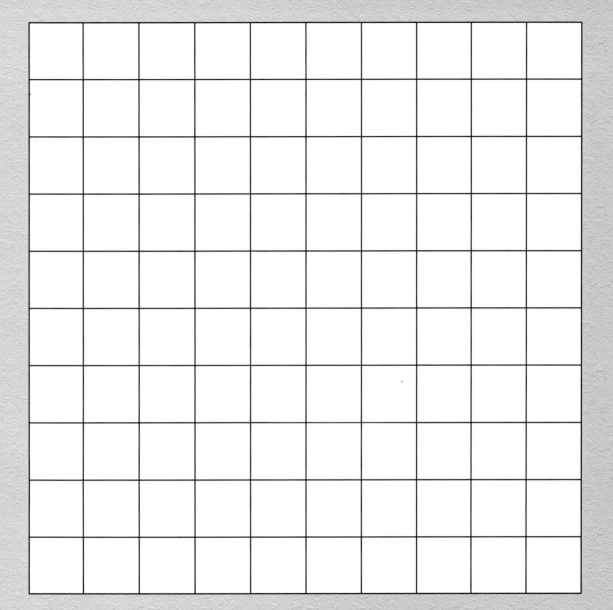

Roman Numeral Secret Message Enlarge 115%

Symmetrical
Butterfly
at 100%

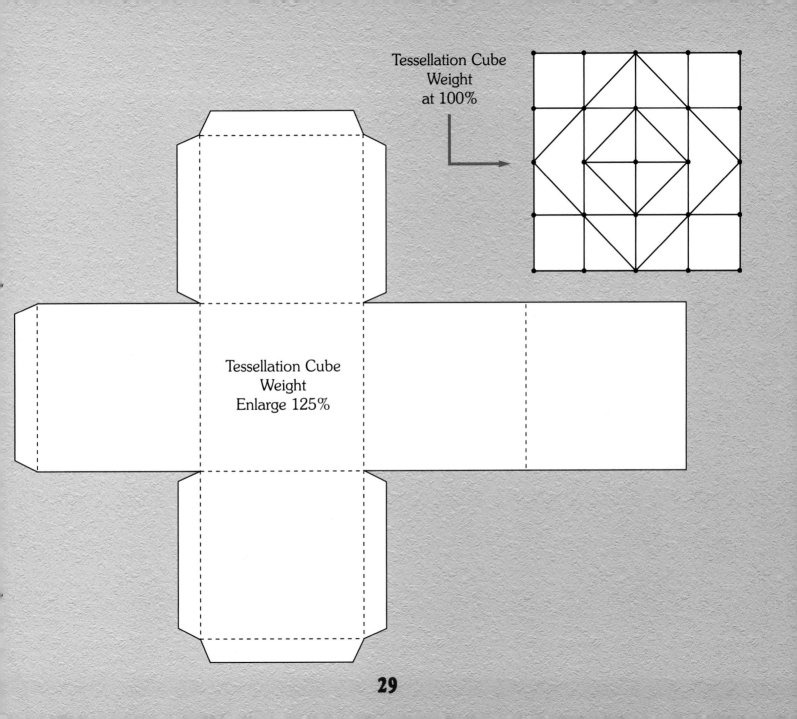

Tessellation Cube
Weight
at 100%

Tessellation Cube
Weight
Enlarge 125%

29

Reading About

Books

Ball, Jonny. *Go Figure!: A Totally Cool Book About Numbers.* New York: DK, 2005.

Long, Lynette. *Measurement Mania: Games and Activities That Make Math Easy and Fun.* New York: Wiley, 2001.

Pistoia, Sara. *Patterns.* Chanhassen, Minn.: Child's World, 2003.

Smolinski, Jill. *The First-Timer's Guide to Origami.* Los Angeles, Calif.: Lowell House Juvenile, 2000.

Tang, Greg. *Math Potatoes: More Mind-Stretching Brain Food.* New York: Scholastic Press, 2005.

Wyatt, Valerie. *The Math Book for Girls and Other Beings Who Count.* Toronto, Canada: Kids Can Press, 2000.

Internet Addresses

Numbers

<http://www.funbrain.com/numbers.html>

Play some fun math games!

Welcome to the World of Aunty Math: Fun Math Challenges for Kids!

<http://www.auntymath.com/>

Learn more about math.

Index